Charles Sutherland

The manual of drill for the use of the Hospital Corps

Charles Sutherland

The manual of drill for the use of the Hospital Corps

ISBN/EAN: 9783742818843

Manufactured in Europe, USA, Canada, Australia, Japa

Cover: Foto ©Suzi / pixelio.de

Manufactured and distributed by brebook publishing software
(www.brebook.com)

Charles Sutherland

The manual of drill for the use of the Hospital Corps

THE

MANUAL OF DRILL

FOR THE· USE OF THE

HOSPITAL CORPS,

U. S. ARMY.

PUBLISHED BY AU

WASH

GOVERNMENT PRINT

1891.

WAR DEPARTMENT,
SURGEON GENERAL'S OFFICE,
WASHINGTON, D. C., *May* 4, 1891.

The following Manual of Drill is adopted and published for the guidance of the Medical Officers and the instruction of the Hospital Corps of the Army of the United States.

CHARLES SUTHERLAND,
Surgeon General.

Approved:

L. A. GRANT,
Acting Secretary of War.

MANUAL OF DRILL

HOSPITAL CORPS, U. S. ARMY.

— — ‑‑   ——

THE DETACHMENT.

1. The detachment is formed in single rank, privates of the Hospital Corps on the right, company bearers on the left, each class graduated in size, the tallest men on the right.

2. The senior hospital steward is on the right of the line; the junior and acting hospital stewards are in the line of file-closers in order of seniority from right to left. The file-closers are posted two yards in rear of the line, and are equally distributed along it. If the detachment is large the second steward may be placed on the left of the line as guide.

TO FORM THE DETACHMENT.

3. The steward, facing the detachment and six yards in front of its center, commands:

FALL IN;

at which the men form in single rank, facing to the right,

4. The steward having sized the men, and having seen that the file-closers are in their proper positions, commands:

Left, FACE;

and calls the roll.

He then commands:

Count, FOURS;

and, facing to the front, salutes the officer in charge, who is in position at a suitable distance in front of the center of the line, reports the result of the roll-call, and then takes his place on the right of the detachment.

5. The steward having saluted, the junior officers take posts. assistant surgeons in the line of file-closers, and surgeons four paces in rear; they distribute themselves equally along the line, in order of seniority from right to left.

The officer then commands:

Right, DRESS; FRONT.

TO MOVE THE DETACHMENT.

6. The detachment having been thus formed may be moved in line or in column of files, of twos or of fours, as follows:

IN LINE.

To march forward, by the commands: (1) *Forward*, (2) *Guide right*, (or *left*), (3) MARCH.

To march backward from a halt: (1) *Backward*, (2) *Guide right* (or *left*), (3) MARCH.

To side step at a halt: (1) *Side step to the right* (or *left*), (2) MARCH, (3) *Detachment*, (4) HALT.

To pass from. quick to double time: (1) *Double time*, (2) MARCH; to resume the quick time: (1) *Quick time*, (2) MARCH.

To change direction during a forward march: (1) *Right* (or *left*) *wheel*, (2) MARCH, and when the desired front has been obtained, (3) *Forward*, (4) MARCH, or if the intended change of direction be slight the command is: *Incline to the right* (or *left*).

In Column of Files.

The detachment being in line at a halt, the column is formed and then moved by the commands: (1) *Right* (or *left*), (2) FACE, (3) *Forward*, (4) MARCH.

If in march, the commands are: (1) *By the right* (or *left*) *flank*, (2) MARCH.

To change direction in march: (1) *Column right* (or *left, or half right or left*), (2) MARCH.

To form line when marching: (1) *By the left* (or *right*) *flank*, (2) MARCH, (3) *Guide right* (or *left*).

To halt and form line: (1) *Detachment*, (2) HALT, (3) *Left* (or *right*), (4) FACE.

Or line may be formed from the column of files by the commands: (1) *Left* (or *right*) *front into line*, (2) MARCH, (3) *Detachment*, (4) HALT, (5) *Left* (or *right*), (6) DRESS, (7) FRONT.

In Column of Twos or Fours.

The column is formed and moved by the commands: (1) *Twos* (or *fours) right* (or *left*), (2) MARCH.

This column changes direction by the commands given above for the column of files.

To change into line: (1) *Twos* (or *fours) left* (or *right*), (2) MARCH, (3) *Detachment*, (4) HALT, (5) *Right* (or *left*), (6) DRESS, (7) FRONT; or line may be formed as from the column of files by the commands: (1) *Left* (or *right*) *front into line*, (2) MARCH, etc.

Or, the column of fours at single rank distance as formed above may be closed to double rank distance: (1) *Double rank distance*, (2) *Double time*, (3) MARCH; and the column thus formed having been marched as required may be spaced to single rank distance by the commands: (1) *Form single rank*, (2) MARCH, after which it is brought into line by: (1) *Fours left* (or *right*), (2) MARCH, (3) *Detachment*, (4) HALT, (5) *Right* (or *left*), (6) DRESS, (7) FRONT.

8

To form column of twos from column of files the commands are: (1) *Form twos*, (2) *Left* (or *right*) *oblique*, (3) MARCH; and the column of twos is reformed into column of files by: (1) *Right* (or *left*) *by file*, (2) MARCH.

7. *To rest the detachment* in any of its formations:

1. *Detachment*, 2. REST.

8. *To resume attention* :

1. *Detachment*, 2. ATTENTION.

9. *To dismiss the detachment:* The officer directs the steward: *Dismiss the detachment*, when the junior officers fall out and the steward commands:

1. *Break ranks*, 2. MARCH.

INSPECTION.

10. The detachment being in line at a halt, the steward draws sword, salutes the surgeon in command, reports and takes his place on the right.

The surgeon then draws sword, and upon the approach of the inspector, the surgeon commands:

Detachment, ATTENTION ;

and salutes the inspector, who acknowledges the salute and directs : *Prepare your detachment for inspection*. The surgeon then commands:

Rear open order, MARCH; FRONT.

11. At the first command, the steward steps briskly three paces to the rear to mark the new alignment of the file-closers, and the surgeon places himself three paces in front of the right file facing to the left. At MARCH, the junior officers step forward, each by the nearest flank, and place themselves opposite their places in line, three paces

in front of the detachment; the men in rank dress to
to the right; the file-closers step backward and align themselves on the steward. The surgeon superintends the
alignment of the junior officers and the rank, and the
steward that of the file-closers ; the surgeon then verifies
the alignment of the file-closers; the junior officers and
file-closers cast their eyes to the front as soon as their
alignment is verified. At FRONT, the steward resumes his
place in rank and the men cast their eyes to the front.

12. From his position on the right of the line of officers
and facing to the left, the surgeon commands:

Draw, KNIFE.

At *draw* each man provided with a knife grasps, and
slightly raises the sheath with the left hand and seizes
the grip with the right, thumb to the rear and against
the guard; at KNIFE he draws the hand quickly and raises
the arm to its full extent at an angle of about forty-five degrees, the knife in a straight line with the arm, then drops
the arm naturally extended by the side, back of blade to
the front, point down. Simultaneously, the junior and
acting stewards draw sword and bring it to a carry.

13. He then commands:

Inspection, ARMS;

and faces to the front. As soon as inspected he returns
sword, and accompanies the inspector. When the latter
begins to inspect the line, the junior officers face about
and stand in place rest.

Commencing on the right, the inspector now proceeds
to minutely inspect the sword or knife, accoutrements,
and dress of each soldier in succession. Each man, as
the inspector approaches him, brings his sword or knife
vertically to the front, raising the hand as high as the
neck and six inches in front of it, edge to the left, the
thumb on the back of the grip; after a slight pause he

turns the wrist outward to show the other side of the
blade, then turns the wrist back, and as the inspector
passes on resumes the original position; after the inspector
has passed he returns sword or knife without command.

14. *To return knife.* each man grasps the sheath with
the left hand, quickly raises up the right hand as high as
the neck and six inches in front of it [as for inspection],
then drops the point of the knife and sheathes the blade.

15. This inspection completed, the surgeon again takes
his post on the right and commands:

Inspection. CASES:

and facing to the front, returns sword, and accompanies
the inspector as before. At CASES the men make a half-face
to the right; those bearing dressing or medicine cases shift
them to the front. the others take their dressing packets in
the right hand, and all face again to the front: as the inspector passes, the cases are opened so as to expose their
contents, and the packets are shown.

After the inspector has passed, each man makes a half-
face to the right. closes and replaces the case or returns
the packet, and faces to the front.

16. If the members of the Hospital Corps are equipped
with blanket-bags, the acting stewards so equipped then
place themselves on the left of the rank; the surgeon,
from his post as before, commands:

1. *Unsling,* 2. BLANKET-BAGS; 3. *Open,* 4. BLANKET-BAGS.

At the first command, each man makes a half-face to the
right and unfastens the hook of the right strap by seizing
the D ring with the thumb and forefinger of the left hand
passed under the blanket-bag; he then unhooks the strap
with the right hand and unslings the blanket-bag by passing the right forearm over the head; at the same time he
faces to the front and. standing erect. holds it by the
strap in front of the knees. At the second command, he
places the blanket-bag on the ground against his toes,

11

the straps underneath, the great-coat outward, and then stands at attention. At the fourth command, he opens the blanket-bag, turning the flap from him, the flap resting on the great-coat; he then stands at attention.

The blanket-bag having been inspected, the surgeon commands:

1. *Repack*, 2. BLANKET-BAGS.

At the second command, each man repacks and fastens up his blanket-bag, leaving it in the same position as before opening it, and then stands at attention.

1. *Sling*, 2. BLANKET-BAGS.

At the command *Sling*, each man grasps the unhooked (right) strap with the right hand, the hooked (left) strap with the left hand, the back of the left hand to the right, raises the blanket-bag, and, standing erect, makes a half-face to the right. At the second command, he swings the blanket-bag over his shoulders, passing the left arm through the hooked strap, and carrying the right-hand strap over the head. He then brings this strap down over the right shoulder, makes a half-face to the left, and hooks the strap with the right hand, holding the D ring with the thumb and forefinger of the left hand, passed under the blanket-bag.

The acting stewards resume their places in line and each man stands at attention.

17. The inspection being completed, the surgeon commands:

Close order, MARCH.

At MARCH the file-closers close to two paces and the junior officers resume their places in line.

18. If there is no junior officer and the detachment is small, the ranks need not be opened, the junior or acting steward, if present, being placed on the right or left of the rank.

12

19. In case any of the members of the detachment are mounted men, their horses and horse equipments will be examined after the inspection of the men dismounted.

MUSTER.

20. All stated musters of the detachment are, when practicable, preceded by a minute and careful inspection.

The detachment being in line with ranks open, the non-commissioned staff officers (if any) place themselves in the line of file-closers, on the left of the stewards, with sword at a carry. The surgeon, upon intimation of the mustering officer, commands:

Draw, KNIFE; *Attention to muster.*

He then returns sword and hands a roll of the Hospital Corps detachment and non-commissioned staff to the mustering officer. The latter calls over the names on the roll; each man, as his name is called, answers "Here" and returns sword or knife. Men without sword or knife are placed on the left, and, after answering, step forward one pace. The muster completed, the ranks are closed and the detachment is dismissed.

21. After muster the presence of the men reported in the hospital or on other duty is verified by the mustering officer, who is accompanied by the surgeon.

LITTER DRILL.

22. For the purposes of litter drill each set of four is a litter squad. The squads are numbered numerically from right to left: if there is an incomplete set, its members are directed to fall out as dummy wounded or for special duty as may be required.

23. No. 1 is chief of squad; No. 4 carries the dressing case.

24. The officer in command will make such changes in the personnel of the sets of four as he deems advisable.

The selection of No. 1 should be determined by the intelligence and experience of the men; No. 4 should be as near in size as possible to No. 1, and No. 2 to No. 3. The fours are then counted again, if necessary. The men having once been placed in this manner should always fall in thereafter in their assigned places.

25. The officer then commands:

Count SQUADS;

when each chief calls out the number of his squad, in numerical order from right to left.

26. Having assigned the medical officers and stewards to appropriate duties, he commands:

Procure litter, MARCH;

when No. 3 of each squad steps one pace to the front, faces as required, proceeds by the nearest route to the litters, takes one, and returning with it on the right shoulder at a slope of at least forty-five degrees, canvas down, resumes his place by passing through his interval a yard to the rear, facing about, and stepping into line.

In procuring, as well as in returning the litters, the men follow each other in the numerical order of their squads.

He may then form the line into column of twos or fours for marching, or may proceed with the instruction of the squads in litter drill.

DRILL WITH THE CLOSED LITTER.

27. To *carry litter* from position in line, the order is given:

Carry, LITTER;

when No. 3 places his left hand upon the litter at the level of the shoulder, and pressing the lower handles backward with the right hand brings the upper handles forward and downward until the litter is in a horizontal position, canvas to the left; meanwhile the other numbers step directly to the front, No. 2 until he is opposite the front handles, which he seizes with his left hand, and Nos. 1 and 4 until they are opposite the center of the litter.

28. The line of litters may be maneuvered by the commands already given [par. 6] to *march forward* or *backward*, to *side-step at a halt*, to *pass from quick to double time or the reverse*, and *to change direction during a march*.

29. *To march to the rear*, a movement which may be occasionally required, the commands are:

To the rear, MARCH;

when all the members execute an *about*, No. 2 left, the others right, the two bearers meanwhile transferring the handles from one hand to the other. On halting, the members face about to the front without command.

30. At a halt, the line of litters *wheels* on the front bearer of the right (or left) squad as a fixed pivot.

31. In changing direction during a forward march, the line *wheels* on the right or left squad as a movable pivot until the desired direction is obtained.

32. A single squad, apart from others, is *faced* as a unit, as follows:

Litter right (or *left*), FACE;

when No. 2 steps off to the right and No. 3 to the left, both describing a quarter of a circle, so as to make the litter revolve horizontally on its center until both face to the right—Nos. 1 and 4 maintain their relative positions opposite the center of the litter.

33. In marching the line by its flank it is converted into a column of litters (single), but this cannot be effected by the commands applicable to men without litters, or with litters at a shoulder, because the front occupied by the squad does not give enough of space to enable each litter to face—a greater interval between the squads is needful.

To face the squads of a detachment so as to march them in column of litters or to increase the intervals between the squads for purposes of drill or service, the commands are:

1. *By the right* (or *left*) *flank*, 2. *Take one yard* (or more) *intervals*, 3. MARCH.

At the second command the first litter faces to the right on a movable center so as to gain sufficient ground, and at MARCH advances in the new direction, each succeeding litter facing in the same manner as soon as its flank is clear and following one yard (or more) in rear of the squad on its right until the last squad has obtained its interval, when the instructor continues the march or halts the command and forms line, as may be desired.

34. If line is to be formed the commands are:

Detachment, HALT; *Left* (or *right*), FACE; or *By the left* (or *right*) *flank*, MARCH; *Detachment*, HALT.

35. The litters being shouldered, par. 47, and rank formed, the squads may be closed again by the commands:

1. *By the right* (or *left*) *flank*, 2. *Close intervals*, 3. MARCH;

when the right squad standing fast, the other squads face to the right, close up and successively halt, and face to the front.

36. The line of litters at close or open intervals may be formed in column of twos by the commands:

Litters, *Twos right* (or *left*), MARCH;

each two wheeling on the front bearer of the right (or left) squad as a pivot.

37. The column may be formed and marched to the front by the commands:

Right (or *left*) *forward*; *Twos right* (or *left*), MARCH.

38. The line formation is recovered by :

Litters, Twos left (or *right*), MARCH; *Litters,* HALT; *Right* (or *left*), DRESS; FRONT.

39. Or by :

Left (or *right*) *front into line,* MARCH; *Litters,* HALT; *Right* (or *left*), DRESS; FRONT.

40. An *about* with the litters at open intervals or in single column is executed by the commands :

Litters, About, FACE ;

when Nos. 2 and 3 step off as in facing to the right, par. 32, but continue the movement until both face to the rear, the other numbers maintaining their relative positions opposite the center of the litter.

41. *To change bearers* the commands are given :

Change Posts, MARCH ;

when No. 1 takes position as No. 3, and No. 4 as No. 2, while Nos. 3 and 2 step to the left and right, respectively, into the vacated positions; the change is effected without halting if in march.

42. The chief of squad continues to exercise command from whatever position he may occupy.

43. When the bearers are again changed the members of the squad resume the positions as at Carry Litter, par. 27.

44. To *ground the litter from the position of carry,* the order is given :

Ground, LITTER ;

when Nos. 2 and 3 lower it to the ground, lengthwise between the files, canvas up.

45. Posts at the grounded litter may at any time be recovered by the commands :

At litter, POSTS ;

when the numbers take posts, No. 2 on the right of the
front handles, No. 3 on the left of the rear handles and
close to them, and Nos. 1 and 4, respectively, on the right
and left of the litter at its midlength and one pace from
it, all facing to the front. This is the invariable position
taken by each number at the above commands, whatever
may have been his previous position or duty.

46. *To carry litter when grounded:* At the commands:

Carry, LITTER;

Nos. 2 and 3 grasp the litter and raise it from the ground
to the position of *carry.*

47. *To shoulder litter from the position of carry:* At the
commands:

Shoulder, LITTER;

No. 2 raises his end to assist No. 3, who places the litter on
his right shoulder, canvas down, supporting it at an angle
of 45 degrees by the right arm and hand; meanwhile the
other numbers step backward and align themselves upon
him in regular order.

48. *To bring the litter to an order from a shoulder:* At the
commands:

Order, LITTER;

No. 3 brings it to a vertical position and drops the lower
handles to the ground, supporting it by the right hand at
the level of the shoulder.

49. *To shoulder litter from the position of order:* At the
commands:

Shoulder, LITTER;

No. 3 grasps the litter with both hands well below its
middle, fingers to the front, and raises it to the shoulder.

50. In the field the litter should always be carried
closed and only opened on reaching the patient.

51. *To open the litter:* At the commands:

Open, LITTER;

the strapped litter, if at a carry, is first lowered to the

28317—2

ground, when Nos. 2 and 3 unbuckle the straps and fasten the free end of each to the pole, then grasp the ends of the right pole with their right hands and rise. This leaves the litter suspended longitudinally, canvas to the left. They then extend the braces, and supporting the litter horizontally by both poles, lower it to the ground and resume the position of attention, each between the handles of his end of the litter.

52. This is the position of the squad when at *litter posts* with the open litter.

53. If the litter be merely folded (that is, unstrapped), it is first brought to a carry, if on the ground, par. 46, when Nos. 2 and 3 drop the left pole, extend the braces, lower the litter, and take position as before.

54. To *close the litter*, the commands are given:

Close, LITTER;

when Nos. 2 and 3 side-step around the handle to the right and left, respectively, face inwards, stoop, and with their right hands raise the litter by the right pole. They then fold the braces and support the closed litter with the hand grasping the lower handles when they face to the front.

55. The litter is strapped by Nos. 2 and 3 at the termination of the exercises.

56. The detachment being in line at a halt, with the litter at a shoulder, at the commands:

Return litter, MARCH;

No. 3 steps one pace to the front, faces as required, and proceeds by the nearest route to the place designated for the litters, where he leaves it, and, returning, resumes his position in line.

DRILL WITH THE OPEN OR LOADED LITTER.

57. *To lift the litter.*—The squad being in position with the men at *litter posts*, par. 52, the commands are given:

Prepare to lift, LIFT.

At the first command Nos. 2 and 3 slip the loops of their slings over the handles, beginning with the left, and grasp the handles; at the second command they rise slowly erect.

58. At the order:

Forward, MARCH;

the bearers step off, No. 2 with the left, No. 3 with the right foot, taking short sliding steps of about 20 inches, to avoid jolting and to secure a uniform motion of the litter. Nos. 1 and 4 step off with the left foot.

59. The so-called single step, which is by far the easiest for the patient, but which is acquired with difficulty, may also be practiced: No. 2 steps off with the left foot and No. 3 follows with his right an instant later and before No. 2 has planted his right; No. 2's right foot next touches the ground, and is immediately followed by No. 3's left.

60. *To lower the litter*, the order is given:

Lower, LITTER;

when Nos. 2 and 3 slowly lower the litter to the ground, release the slings from the handles, and stand erect.

61. The open litter should be lifted and lowered slowly and without jerk, both ends simultaneously, the rear bearer moving in accord with the front bearer, so as to maintain the canvas horizontal; in fact the open litter should be handled for purposes of drill as if it were a loaded litter.

62. For drill with the loaded litter dummy patients are directed to lie down wherever required, and each squad is separately exercised in loading, marching, passing obstacles, unloading, etc., under the orders of its chief or an instructor.

63. *To cease drilling and re-form the detachment*, the officer in command directs the first squad to resume its original position in line with loaded litter, whereupon the other squads at once proceed, in numerical order, to their places in line with loaded litter; the patients are then directed to rise and fall out.

TO LOAD THE LITTER.

64. The litters being lifted, par. 57, or at a carry, pars. 27, 46, at the commands:

Take post to load, MARCH;

each chief assumes entire charge of his squad, and proceeds independently. The squad advances toward its assigned patient and halts one yard from his head or feet, preferably his head, and in a line with his body. The litter is now opened (if it has been carried closed, as is the rule in field service, par. 50) and lowered.

65. The chief of squad then commands:

Stand to patient, right (or *left*), MARCH.

66. With litter at the head of the patient, if the command is right, Nos. 2, 1, and 3, proceeding by the right, take position, No. 2 at the right knee, No. 1 at the right hip, and No. 3 at the right shoulder, while No. 4, passing by the left, takes position by the left hip opposite No. 1, all facing the patient.

67. If the command is left, Nos. 2, 4, and 3, proceeding by the left, take position, No. 2 at the left knee, No. 4 at the left hip, and No. 3 at the left shoulder, while No. 1, passing by the right, takes position by the right hip opposite No. 4, all facing the patient.

68. Should the litter be placed at the feet of the patient, Nos. 1 and 4 cross each other on their way to their respective sides of the patient.

69. It will be seen from the above that, whether the command is right or left, the positions of Nos. 1 and 4 are invariable, No. 1 at the right hip, No. 4 at the left hip, and that the positions of Nos. 2 and 3 are always at the knee and shoulder, respectively, on the right or left of

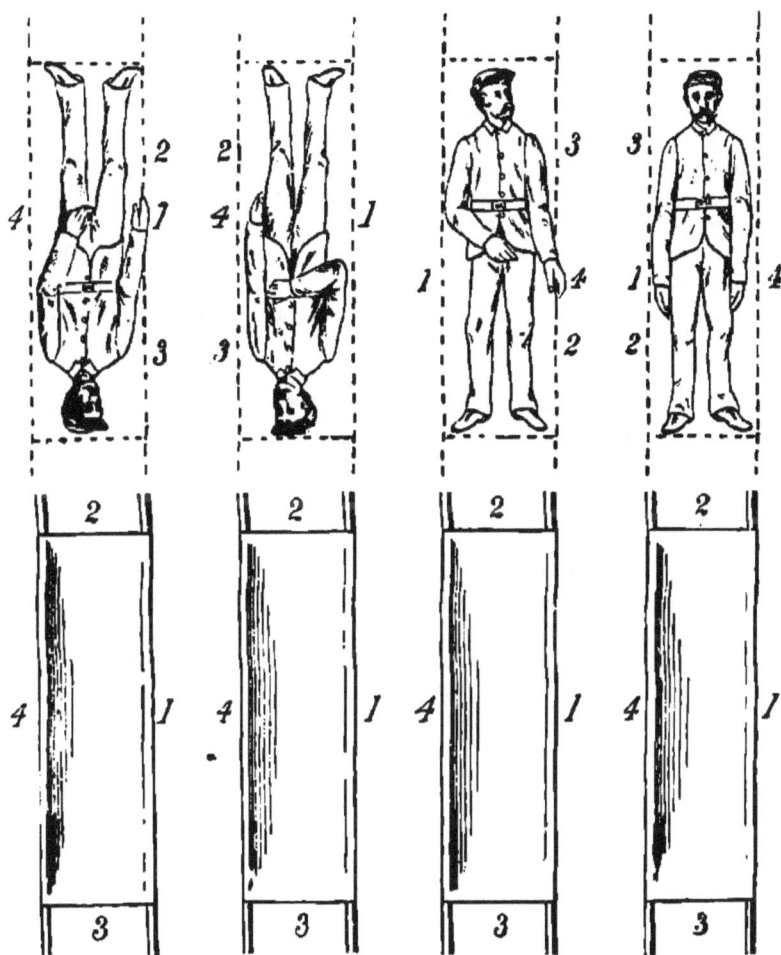

STANDING TO WOUNDED BY THE RIGHT OR LEFT.

It will be observed that when No. 1 or 4 has placed the litter by the knees of the three bearers, and the patient has been lowered, every member of the squad is in his proper position for marching off; No. 2 at the feet, No. 3 at the head, and Nos. 1 and 4 on the right and left respectively.

the patient, as the command may be; if right, they are on each side of No. 1; if left, they are on each side of No. 4.

70. In field service, Nos. 1 and 4 should run ahead and take position at the hip on their respective sides; they remove the arms and accouterments of the wounded man and examine him to determine the site and nature of the injury; and having administered restoratives, if required, and applied such dressings or splints as are needful or available, in which duty all the members of the squad may be made use of, the chief of squad commands: *Stand to patient*, etc., par. 65.

71. As a rule, the command should be right or left, according as the right or left side of the patient is injured, so that by having the three bearers on that side a better support may be given to the wounded parts.

Prepare to lift.

72. At this command all the bearers kneel on the right knee if on the right of the patient, and on the left knee if on his left. No. 2 passes both arms under the patient's legs, carefully supporting the fracture, if there be one. Nos. 1 and 4 pass their arms under his hips and thighs side by side, not locking hands. No. 3 passes one arm under his neck to the further armpit, with the other supporting the nearer shoulder.

LIFT.

73. At this command all lift together slowly and carefully and place the patient upon their knees. As soon as the patient is firmly supported there, the bearer on the free side (No. 1 or 4) relinquishes his hold, passes quickly and by the shortest line to the litter, which he takes up by the middle, one pole in each hand, and returning rapidly places it under the patient and against the bearer's ankles.

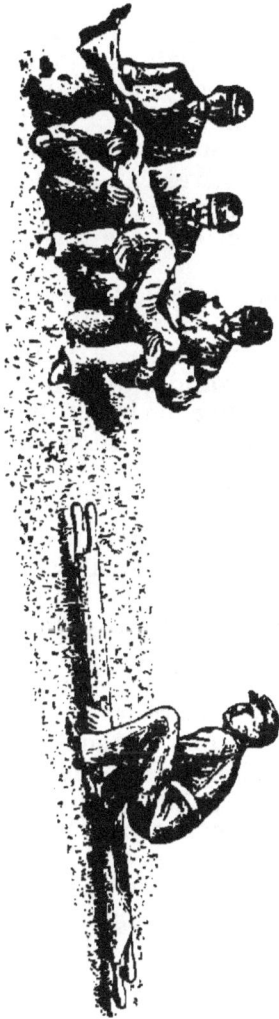

LIFTING THE PATIENT, PAR. 73.

Lower, PATIENT.

74. The free bearer, No. 1 or 4. stoops and assists the other members in gently and carefully lowering the patient upon the litter. The bearers then rise and at once resume their positions at litter posts, par 52.

75. In the field when the ground on which the patient lies is such that the litter cannot be placed directly under him, it should be placed as near to him as possible and preferably in a direction parallel to, or in a line with, the body.

76. It may sometimes be necessary to carry the patient to the litter instead of the litter to the patient. The bearers having secured their hold, as before described, par. 72, rise together and move slowly and steadily to the litter. If the distance be great it will be best for Nos. 1 and 4 to interlock fingers, palms up.

POSITION OF PATIENT ON THE LITTER.

77. The position of a patient on the litter depends on the character of his injury. An overcoat, blanket, blanket-bag, knapsack, or other suitable and convenient article, should be used as a pillow to give support and a slightly raised position to the head. If the patient is faint the head should be kept low. Difficulty of breathing in wounds of the chest is relieved by a sufficient padding underneath. In wounds of the abdomen the best position is on the injured side, or on the back if the front of the abdomen is wounded, the legs in either case being drawn up, and a pillow or other available object placed under the knees to keep them bent.

78. In an injury of the upper extremity, calling for litter transportation, the best position is on the back with the injured arm laid over the body or suitably placed by its side, or on the uninjured side with the wounded arm laid over the body. In injuries of the lower extremity the patient should be on his back, or inclining toward the wounded side: in cases of fracture of either lower extremity, if a splint cannot be applied, it is always well to bind both limbs together.

79. The litter having been brought to a halt and lowered, the order is given:

Change posts, MARCH;

when Nos. 1 and 4 relieve the bearers, as in par. 41.

80. The position of the men under this order holds good until posts are again changed, except in the case of such a disarrangement of the squad as calls for its reformation by the commands: *At litter,* POSTS, when all take position in accordance with the requirements of par. 52.

GENERAL DIRECTIONS.

81. In moving the patient either with or without litter every movement should be made without haste and as gently as possible, having special care not to jar the injured part. The command: *Steady,* will be used to prevent undue haste or other irregular movements.

82. The loaded litter should never be raised nor lowered without orders.

83. The rear bearer should watch the movements of the front bearer and time his own by them, so as to insure ease and steadiness of action.

84. The number of steps per minute will depend on the weight carried and other conditions affecting each individual case.

85. The handles of the litter should be held in the hands supported by the slings at arms-length, and only under the most exceptional conditions should the handles be supported on the shoulders.

86. The bearers should keep the litter level, notwithstanding any unevenness of the ground.

87. In making ascents the rear handles should be raised to bring the litter to the proper level, and if the ascent is steep No. 1 should come to the assistance of No. 3 in raising it to the shoulder if necessary.

88. In making descents the front handles should be raised, and if the descent is steep No. 4 should aid No. 2 in raising them.

89. As a rule the patient should be carried on the litter feet foremost, but in going up hill his head should be in front; in case of fracture of the lower extremities he is carried up hill feet foremost and down hill head foremost to prevent the weight of the body from pressing down on the injured part.

90. For purposes of drill a tag of red or white cotton or flannel may be attached to dummy wounded to indicate the site and character of the injuries to be cared for.

TO PASS OBSTACLES.

91. A breach should be made in a fence or wall for the passage of the litter if there be no gate or other opening; but should it be necessary to surmount the obstacle, Nos. 4 and 1 take hold of the poles each on his own side, thus permitting No. 2 to get over, when the front handles are passed to him; Nos. 4 and 1 then follow, and taking hold near the rear handles support the litter until No. 3 has crossed. All then resume their positions and continue the march.

92. The passage of a deep cut or ditch is effected in a similar manner; Nos. 1 and 4 bestride or descend into the cut and support the litter near its front handles until No. 2 has crossed and resumed his hold, when they then give support near the rear handles until No. 3 has crossed.

93. If the cut or ditch be wide, the litter is halted and lowered with the front handles (or feet) near the edge; Nos. 4 and 2 descend and advance the litter, keeping it level, until the rear handles (or feet) rest upon the edge, when Nos. 3 and 1, who have assisted in this movement, descend and resume the support of their respective handles; the ascent on the other side is made by Nos. 4 and 2 resting their handles on the edge, ascending and advancing the litter until its rear handles rest upon the edge, when 3 and 1 ascend and the march is resumed.

94. In crossing a running stream or broken or otherwise difficult ground Nos. 1 and 4 give support on their respective sides of the litter or take full care each of the handle of his own side, No. 4 in front, No. 1 in rear. In the latter case the commands would be: *By four*, Carry Litter.

TO LOAD WITH REDUCED NUMBERS.

95. Should only three bearers be available, the litter is placed as usual at the head of the patient, Nos. 2 and 3 proceed to their proper positions at the knee and shoulder of one side, while No. 1 stands at the hip of the opposite side. The patient, having been lifted by the three bearers, is supported on the knees of Nos. 2 and 3, while No. 1 places the litter in position under him.

96. Another method for three bearers, when it is necessary to carry the patient to the litter, is as follows:

Nos. 2 and 3 take position opposite the knee and hip, respectively, while No. 1 stands by the hip opposite No. 3. As with four bearers, Nos. 2 and 3 should preferably be directed to the wounded side. At the usual commands, Nos. 1 and 3 stoop and, raising the patient to a sitting position, place each one arm and hand around the back and interlock the fingers of the other hand, palms up, under the upper part of the thighs. The patient, if able, clasps his arms around their necks. No. 2 supports the lower extremities with both arms passed under them, one above, the other below, the knee.

97. If only two bearers are available (Nos. 2 and 3), the patient is necessarily always carried to the litter; No. 2 proceeds by the right and No. 3 by the left and take

METHOD FOR THREE BEARERS, PAR. 96.

position on opposite sides of the patient near his hips. They lift patient as directed, par. 96, for Nos. 1 and 3, the legs remaining unsupported, and carry him head foremost over the near end and length of the litter.

98. In case of a fractured lower extremity, the two bearers must take hold of the patient on the injured side, No. 2 supporting both lower extremities, while No. 3 supports the body, the patient clasping his arms around his neck.

TO UNLOAD THE LITTER.

99. To unload with four or three men, they *stand to patient* as in loading; at the commands: *Prepare to lift*, LIFT, they raise him upon the knees, the free bearer removes the litter, and at *Lower*, PATIENT, they lower him carefully to the ground.

100. With two men, they form a two-handed seat and lift the patient off the litter; or, in case of fracture, they stand on the same side and, stooping, lift him and take two steps backward to clear the litter, when they lower him to the ground.

TO TRANSFER PATIENT FROM LITTER TO BED OR ANOTHER LITTER.

101. With four men, the litter being placed close along side the bed (on either side), the patient's head corresponding to that of the bed, he is taken from the litter and supported on the knees in the usual manner. The free bearer then removes the litter, and the others having risen take a step forward and lower the patient upon the bed.

102. With three men, the litter is placed at the foot of the bed, and in line with it; the three bearers, all on one side, lift the patient without kneeling and move cautiously by side steps to the bedside.

103. With two men, the litter is placed at the foot of the bed as before, and the patient carried cautiously by side steps or carried head foremost over the foot of the bed on a two-handed seat.

IMPROVISATION OF LITTERS.

104. Many objects can be used for this purpose:
Camp cots, window blinds, doors, benches, boards, ladders, etc., properly padded.

Litters may be made with sacks or bags of any description, if large and strong enough, by ripping the bottoms and passing two poles through them and tying cross pieces to the poles to keep them apart; two, or even three, sacks placed end to end on the same poles may be necessary to make a safe and comfortable litter.

Bed-ticks are used in the same way by slipping the poles through holes made by snipping off the four corners.

Pieces of matting, rug, or carpet trimmed into shape may be fastened to poles by tacks or twine.

Straw mats, leafy twigs, weeds, hay, straw, etc., covered or not with a blanket, will make a good bottom over a framework of poles and cross sticks.

Better still is a litter with bottom of ropes or raw-hide strips whose turns cross each other at close intervals.

105. But the usual military improvisation is by means of two rifles and a blanket.

One-half of the blanket is rolled lengthwise into a cylinder, which is placed along the back of the patient, who has been turned carefully on his side. The patient is then turned over on to the blanket and the cylinder unrolled on the other side. The rifles (with bayonets fixed, if at hand) are then laid on the ground under the side edges of the blanket, muzzles to the front and somewhat converging, butts to the rear or head of the patient, and are rolled tightly in the blanket, each a like number of rolls, until the side of the body of the patient is reached, when they are turned hammers downward.

Two bearers may carry the wounded man in this improvisation, but it is better, whenever possible, that four men should do so—two on each side, firmly grasping the blanket over the rifle.

METHODS OF REMOVING WOUNDED WITHOUT LITTERS.

FOR ONE BEARER.

106. While it is not desirable that one bearer should, ordinarily, be required or permitted to lift a patient unassisted, emergencies may arise when a knowledge of proper methods of lifting and carrying by one bearer is of the utmost value.

107. A single bearer may carry a patient in his arms, on his back, or across his shoulder.

To bring the patient into any of these positions, the first steps are as follows:

The bearer, turning patient on his face, steps astride body, facing towards the head, and with hands in his armpits lifts him to his knees, then clasping hands over the abdomen, lifts him to his feet and places the patient's left arm around his (the bearer's) neck, the patient's left side resting against his body.

108. From this position the bearer proceeds as follows:

To.lift the patient in his arms:

The bearer, with his right arm behind patient's back, passes his left under thighs and lifts him into position.

To place patient astride of back:

109. The bearer shifts himself to the front of patient, back to him, stoops, and grasping his legs above the knees brings him well up on his back.

To place patient across back:

110. The bearer with his left hand seizes the right arm of the patient and draws it down upon his left shoulder,

BY ONE BEARER ASTRIDE OF BACK, PAR. 109.

then, shifting himself in front, stoops and clasps the right thigh with his right arm passed between the legs, when he rises.

To place patient across shoulder:

111. The bearer faces patient, stoops, places his right shoulder against the abdomen, and clasps the right thigh with the right arm passed between the legs: he then grasps the patient's right hand with his left, and draws the right arm down upon his left shoulder until the wrist is seized by his own right hand; lastly, he, with his left hand, grasps the patient's left and steadies it against his side, when he rises.

112. In lowering patient from these positions the motions are reversed. Should a patient be wounded in such manner as to require these motions to be conducted from his right side, instead of left, as laid down, the change is simply one of hands—the motions proceed as directed, substituting right for left, and *vice versa*.

FOR TWO BEARERS.

By the two-handed seat:

113. The patient lying on the ground, at the command:

Form two-handed seat,

the bearers take position facing each other, No. 1 on the right and No. 2 on the left of the patient near his hips.

Prepare to lift.

They raise the patient to a sitting posture, pass each one hand and arm around his back, while the other hands are passed under the thighs, palms up, and the fingers interlocked. At the command:

LIFT,

both rise together. If the patient has to be so carried for a

28317—3

BY ONE BEARER ACROSS SHOULDERS, PAR. 111.

long distance, the bearers should grasp each other's wrists
under the patient's thighs. In marching the bearers
should break step, the right bearer starting with the
right foot and the left bearer with the left foot.

By the four-handed seat:

114. This method is applicable when the patient has
considerable strength and the use of his arms. At the
command:

Form four-handed seat,

the two bearers take position as in par. 113. At *Prepare
to lift,* they stoop, pass their hands under the patient's
buttocks and form a four-handed seat, each bearer grasping his right forearm just above the wrist with the left
hand, and then grasping the other bearer's disengaged
forearm with his own disengaged hand, palms down. At
the command LIFT, both rise together, the patient steady-
ing himself by passing his arms around the bearers' necks.

By the extremities:

115. This method requires no effort on the part of the
patient; but it is not applicable to severe injuries of the
lower extremities. One bearer stands by the patient's
head, the other between his legs, both facing towards the
feet. At *Prepare to lift,* the rear bearer clasps the wounded
man around the body under the arms, while the front
bearer passes his arms from the outside under the flexed
knees. At LIFT, both bearers rise together.

By the rifle seat:

116. A good seat may be made by running the barrels
of two rifles through the sleeves of an overcoat, so that
the coat lies back up, collar to the rear. The front bearer
rolls the tails tightly around the barrels and takes his

METHOD BY TWO BEARERS, PAR. 115.

grasp over them; the rear bearer holds by the butts, hammers down.

117. A stronger seat is secured when the gun-slings are used. The slings are unhooked and let out to their full length from the rear swivel. The rifles are then placed upon the ground, parallel to each other, but with the hammers outside, at a distance of about 20 inches. Each sling is passed around the opposite rifle, then around its own,

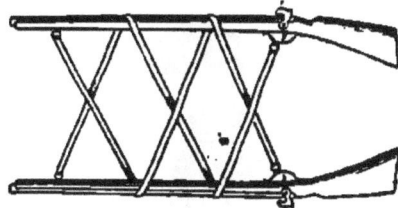

THE RIFLE SEAT.

and lastly hooked to the front swivel of the other rifle, thus forming a seat 20 inches wide and 2 feet long. on which the patient sits with his back against the rear bearer, his legs hanging over outside, and the hollow of his knees resting upon the barrels.

118. A quicker way to prepare a rifle seat, when a twist of the slings is not objectionable, is as follows:*

Two men with the slings of their rifles loosened, as for carrying on the back, face each other and bring their pieces to a "present arms." Thereupon No. 1 seizes the sling of No. 2's rifle with the right hand, lifts his own rifle with the left hand, and passes the butt through the sling from left to right, straightening the piece as soon as the hammer has cleared the sling. No. 2 grasps the sling of No. 1's rifle with the right hand, and, depressing the muzzle of his own piece, passes it through the sling he holds, from left to right, straightening the piece as the sling is cleared.

The pieces now being at the original "present," the butts are lowered to the ground, the left hand of each man being brought to the muzzle of his gun. No. 2 grasps the muzzles, No. 1 stoops and secures the butts.

* Method of Captain Norton Strong, U. S. A.

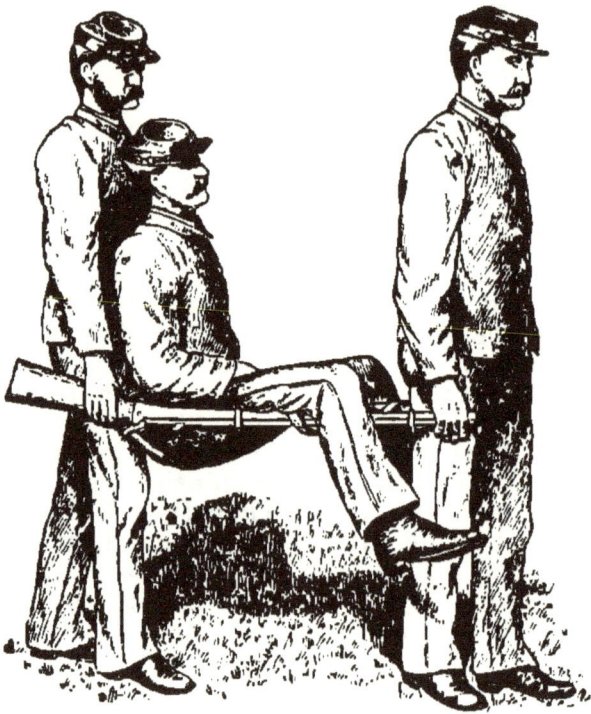

THE RIFLE SEAT, PAR. 117.

FOR THREE BEARERS.

119. See paragraphs 95 and 96.

TO PLACE A SICK OR WOUNDED MAN ON HORSEBACK.

120. In emergencies it may be needful to carry a disabled man on horseback. The help required to mount him will depend on the site and nature of his injuries; in many cases he is able to help himself materially. If he be entirely helpless, five men are required to get him into the saddle—one to hold the horse, the others to act as bearers.

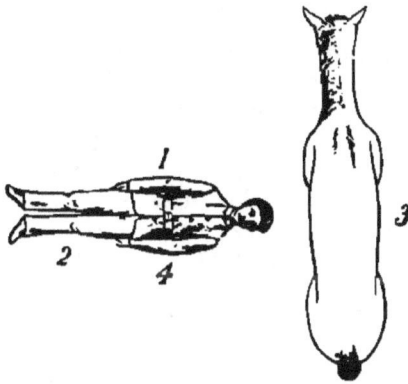

The horse, blind-folded, is held in position at right angles to the patient, who lies on the ground on his back on the near side, with his head towards the horse. Nos. 2, 1, and 4 take position as at *stand*

TO PLACE THE PATIENT ON HORSEBACK.

to patient by the left, No. 2 at the ankles on the left, and the others at the right and left hip, respectively, while No. 3 stands on the off side of the horse ready to grasp the shoulders of the patient when they are brought within his reach. At *Prepare to Lift*, No. 2 passes both arms under the legs; 1 and 4 place each one hand under the corresponding buttock and the other under the shoulders, not locking hands. At LIFT, the patient is carefully raised and carried over the horse until his seat reaches the saddle. No. 1 now goes quickly around the horse's head to the off side and the patient is made to pivot in the saddle, Nos. 3 and 4 on either side supporting and at the same time depressing his back while No. 2 raises the legs unti! the right leg comes within reach of No. 1, when each foot is carried downward for support in its stirrup.

121. To dismount, the process is reversed : Nos. 3 and 4, standing on each side of the horse, depress the body of the patient backward while 1 and 2 raise the legs. The patient is then pivoted to the left, No. 1 passing the right leg over the pommel to No. 2 and then taking position on the near side to lower the patient to the ground or litter, as the case may be.

122. *To mount with the assistance of three men :* The three bearers take position by the patient, as above, on the near side of the horse and raise him into the saddle, when, if the legs are not injured, No. 2 relinquishes them to take post on the off side and aid No. 1 in adjusting them ; but, if the legs are injured, No. 1 should take post on the off side to aid No 2 in this part of the work, the other member of the squad meanwhile supporting the body in the saddle.

123. *With only two bearers* it is possible, but difficult, to place a helpless man on horseback : The patient having been raised into the saddle by both bearers, one of them goes to the off side to aid in effecting his adjustment.

124. The patient once mounted should be made as safe and comfortable as possible. A comrade may be mounted behind him to hold him and guide the horse ; otherwise, a lean-back must be provided, made of a blanket roll, a pillow, or a bag filled with leaves or grass. If the patient be very weak, the lean-back can be made of a sapling bent into an arch over the cantle of the saddle, its ends securely fastened, or of some other framework to which the patient is bound.

THE TRAVOIS.

125. The travois consists of a litter drawn by one animal, the rear handles trailing on the ground. It is the ordinary Indian conveyance for patients and baggage, and being such may be considered the best method of

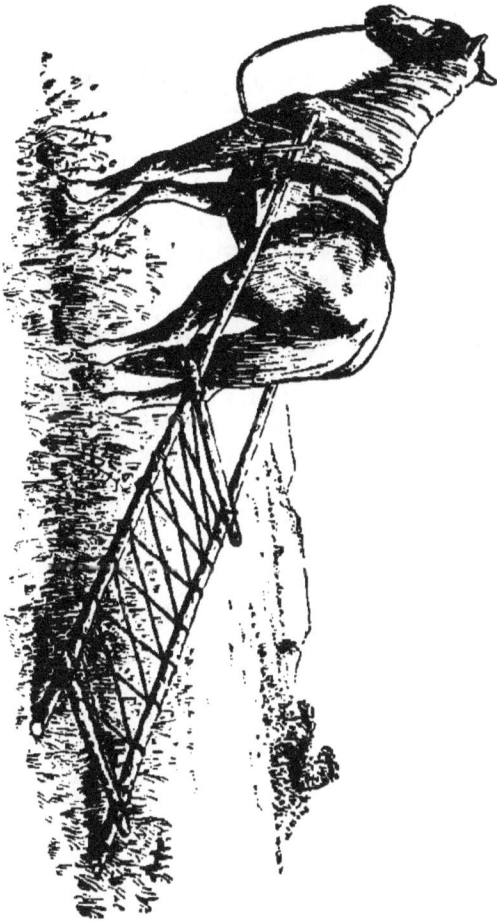

THE TRAVOIS, PAR. 125.

improvising means of transport in our western country. The travois requires only one animal and two men, one to lead the animal, the other to watch the litter and be ready to lift its rear poles when passing over obstacles, crossing streams, or going up hill.

It may be improvised by cutting poles about 15 feet long and 2 inches in diameter at the small end. These poles are laid parallel to each other, small ends to the front and 2½ feet apart; the large ends about 3 feet apart, and one of them projecting 8 or 10 inches beyond the other. The poles are connected by a crossbar about 6 feet from the front ends and another about 2½ feet from the shorter rear end, each notched at its ends and securely lashed by its notches to the poles. Between the cross-pieces the litter-bed, 6½ feet long, is filled in with canvas, blanket, etc., securely fastened to the poles and crossbars, or with rope, lariat, rawhide strips, etc., stretching obliquely from pole to pole in many turns crossing each other to form the basis for a light mattress or improvised bed; or a litter may be made fast between the poles to answer the same purpose. The front ends of the poles are then securely fastened to the saddle of the animal.

THE TWO-HORSE LITTER.

126. The *two-horse litter* consists of a litter with long handles used as shafts for carriage by two horses, or mules, one in front the other in rear of the litter. It accommodates one recumbent patient. On a good trail it is preferable to the travois, as the patient lies in the horizontal position, and, in case of fractured limbs, they can easily be secured against disturbance. The great disadvantage of this litter is, that it requires two animals and three men for the carriage of each patient, one to attend to the disabled man and the others to watch over and guide the movements of the animals. This litter may be improvised in the same manner as the travois, only the poles should be 16½ feet long, and the crossbars forming the ends of the litter-bed should be fastened 5 feet from the front and rear ends of the poles. The ends are made fast to the saddles by notches, into which the fastening ropes are securely tied.

4

AMBULANCE DRILL.

127. The regulation ambulance provides transportation for eight men sitting, or two lying. As prepared for the road it should contain two closed litters beneath the seats, with spare litters outside, and four seats for two occupants apiece.

128. The litters are said to be *packed* when they are closed and placed beneath the seats, canvas up. The seats are said to be *prepared* when they are horizontal with the leg-irons resting on the floor-plates; and *packed* when they are hooked against the sides of the wagon.

129. *To take posts at the ambulance,* the squad is marched to the ambulance preferably by column of files, and when within a short distance of it the commands are given:

At ambulance, POSTS,

when No. 1 takes post on the left, No 2 in the center, and No. 3 on the right of the rear of the ambulance and close to it, No. 4 on the right of No. 3.

130. This is the invariable position of the squad *at ambulance posts;* and when disarranged, from whatever cause, it may be reassembled by these commands for service at the ambulance.

131. The ambulance having litters and seats packed, *to prepare seats:*

The ambulance being at a halt and the squad at ambu lance posts, the commands are given:

Prepare, SEATS.

Nos. 1 and 3 raise the curtain if necessary and open the tail-gate: Nos. 2 and 3 enter the ambulance, No. 2 facing the front and No. 3 the rear seat of their respective sides. Each man seizes the lower edge of the seat about six inches from the ends with both hands and lifts it carefully to free the hooks from the upper slots, and then slips them into the lower slots; he raises the legs and adjusts them to the seat which he tries for firmness before leaving it. He then prepares in like manner the other seat of his side.

132. When the seats are prepared, No. 2 leaves the ambulance, but No. 3 remains, unless otherwise directed, until he has stowed such baggage as may be passed to him by the other bearers; they now resume their places at ambulance posts.

TO PACK SEATS.

133. The ambulance being at a halt and the squad at ambulance posts, the commands are:

Pack, SEATS.

Nos. 1 and 3 raise the curtain, open the tail-gate, and each removes the litter on his own side, laying it on the ground two yards in rear; Nos. 2 and 3 enter the ambulance, No. 2 facing the front and No. 3 the rear seat of their respective sides. Each man holds the seat with one hand and folds the leg-irons with the other; then seizing the front of the seat with both hands he raises the seat to clear the hooks from the lower slots and slips them into the upper slots. He then packs in like manner the other seat of his side.

134. As soon as the seats are packed the bearers resume their places at ambulance posts.

135. Should it be necessary to pack seats while the ambulance is in motion, the tail-gate is opened, Nos. 2 and 3 enter, pass out the litters to Nos. 1 and 4, respectively, and pack the seats as described.

TO LOAD THE AMBULANCE.

136. The litter being lifted, at the commands:

Take post to load ambulance, MARCH,

the squad proceeds to the ambulance, and when one yard from the rear step, halts and faces the litter about, so that the head of the patient is towards the rear of the ambulance, and then lower it.

137. At the command:

Prepare to load,

Nos. 2 and 3 face about (towards the ambulance) and Nos. 1 and 4 face the litter; No. 3 steps outside of his right handle and faces the litter. No. 2 remains between the rear handles, and No. 1 takes post outside the left handle opposite No. 3 and facing him, while No. 4 opens the tail-gate and sees that the ambulance is in suitable condition for the reception of the patient. If he requires assistance No. 1 should render it.

At the command:

LOAD,

the three bearers, Nos. 1, 2, and 3, stoop, grasp their respective handles and slowly raise the litter to the level of the floor of the ambulance and advance to it, being careful to keep the litter in a horizontal position; the legs are placed on the floor by Nos. 1 and 3 and the litter pushed in by No. 2, assisted by the others. When this is accomplished, Nos. 1, 2, and 3 are in position at ambulance posts, No. 1 on the left, No. 2 in the center, and No. 3 on the right, facing the rear of the ambulance and close to it. Nos. 1 and 3 fasten the tail-gate; No. 4 places in the forward compartment the arms and accouterments of the patient (if any) and then takes his position on the right. After this No. 1, having seen that everything is secure, faces the men about and marches them off to continue the drill by bringing up another loaded litter, returning to unload, etc.

TO UNLOAD THE AMBULANCE.

138. The squad having been brought to ambulance posts, the order is given:

Prepare to unload,

when Nos. 1 and 3 open the tail-gate and No. 2 lays hold of the projecting handles. At the command:

UNLOAD,

No. 2 draws out the litter, Nos. 1 and 3, facing inward, support the poles until the front handles are reached. The litter, carefully supported in a horizontal position, is then lowered with the head of the patient one yard in rear of the wagon; No. 4 closes the tail-gate, and all take position at litter posts. The litter is then lifted and carried in the required direction.

139. At the conclusion of the drill with ambulances the detachment is re-formed in line of litters as in par. 63.

○

www.ingramcontent.com/pod-product-compliance
Lightning Source LLC
Chambersburg PA
CBHW021548270326
41930CB00008B/1417